Cambridge Colonial Club

The Charter and By-Laws of the Colonial Club of Cambridge

With a List of the Officers and Members

Cambridge Colonial Club

The Charter and By-Laws of the Colonial Club of Cambridge
With a List of the Officers and Members

ISBN/EAN: 9783337232993

Printed in Europe, USA, Canada, Australia, Japan

Cover: Foto ©Suzi / pixelio.de

More available books at **www.hansebooks.com**

THE

CHARTER AND BY-LAWS
OF THE COLONIAL CLUB
OF CAMBRIDGE

*WITH A LIST OF THE OFFICERS
AND MEMBERS*

CLUB HOUSE 20 QUINCY STREET

CAMBRIDGE
Printed at the Riverside Press
1894

No. 4074.

Commonwealth of Massachusetts.

BE IT KNOWN that whereas T. W. Higginson, James J. Myers, Henry H. Gilmore, Charles W. Eliot, Alvin F. Sortwell, Joseph G. Thorp, Jr., C. W. Kingsley, Henry P. Walcott, William A. Munroe, Charles J. McIntire, Daniel U. Chamberlin, Edmund Reardon, and Edmund A. Whitman have associated themselves with the intention of forming a corporation under the name of THE COLONIAL CLUB, for the purpose of establishing and maintaining a place for a reading-room, library, and social intercourse, and have complied with the provisions of the Statutes of this Commonwealth in such case made and provided, as appears from the certificate of the President, Treasurer, and Directors of said corporation, duly approved by the Commissioner of Corporations, and recorded in this office.

NOW, THEREFORE, I, Henry B. Peirce, Secretary of the Commonwealth of Massachusetts, do hereby certify that said T. W. Higginson, J. J. Myers, H. H. Gilmore, C. W. Eliot, A. F. Sortwell, J. G. Thorp, Jr., C. W. Kingsley, H. P. Walcott, W. A. Munroe, C. J. McIntire, D. U. Chamberlin, E. Reardon and E. A. Whitman, their associates and successors, are legally organized and established as and are hereby made an existing corporation under the name of THE COLONIAL CLUB, with the powers, rights, and privileges, and subject to the limitations, duties, and restrictions which by law appertain thereto.

{ SEAL } WITNESS my official signature hereunto subscribed, and the seal of the Commonwealth of Massachusetts hereunto affixed this fourteenth day of April in the year of our Lord one thousand eight hundred and ninety.

HENRY B. PEIRCE,
Secretary of the Commonwealth.

PRESIDENTS,

WITH DATES OF THEIR ELECTION.

———

BY-LAWS

ARTICLE I.

GOVERNMENT.

SECTION 1. The officers of the Club shall be a President, four Vice-Presidents, a Secretary (who shall be Clerk of the Corporation), a Treasurer, and nine Directors, who with the President and Secretary shall be an Executive Committee ; a Committee on Admissions, and an Auditing Committee.

The officers shall be elected by ballot at the annual meeting in each year, and shall serve until their successors shall have been elected.

SECTION 2. The President, or, in his absence, the Vice-President senior in order of election, and present, shall preside at all meetings of the Club. In the absence of the President and all the Vice-Presidents, a presiding officer shall be chosen without ballot from the members of the Club. The President and Secretary shall be, *ex officio*, chairman and secretary of the Executive Committee.

SECTION 3. The Secretary shall keep a

record of the proceedings of the Club and of the Executive Committee, and of all matters of which a record shall be deemed advisable by the Club or by said committee, in books belonging to the Club. The records of the Secretary shall, at all reasonable times, be open to the inspection of any member of the Club. It shall be the duty of the Secretary to notify members of their election, to keep a roll of the members of the Club, to issue notices for all business meetings of the Club at least five days previous to such meetings (with a brief mention of the business to be transacted when a special meeting is called), and to conduct the correspondence. He shall also be the keeper of the seal and of all documents of the Club. He shall be exempt from payment of the annual assessment.

SECTION 4. The Treasurer shall collect, and, under the direction of the Executive Committee, disburse all moneys of the Club. He shall keep the accounts of the Club in books belonging to it, which shall be at all times open to the inspection of the Executive Committee and Auditing Committee ; he shall report in writing at each quarterly meeting of the Executive Committee the balance of money on hand, and the outstanding obligations of the Club, as far as practicable ; and he shall make a full report, at the Annual Meeting of the Club, of the receipts and disbursements of the past year, with such suggestions as to the financial management of the Club as he may deem proper. He shall turn over immediately, to his successor, all the money, books, vouchers, and other property in his hands belonging to the Club. He shall be exempt from the payment of the annual assessment.

SECTION 5. The Executive Committee shall have the management and control of the Club and of its property, and shall exercise a general superintendence over its interests and affairs. They may make and authorize all necessary purchases and contracts, but shall have no power to make the Club liable for any debt beyond the amount of money which shall, at the time of contracting such debt, be in the Treasurer's hands and not needed for the discharge of prior debts or liabilities. They shall have the power to make such regulations as they shall think proper ; and, generally, to do all things which may be necessary for the management of its concerns. They shall always be subject to such instructions and limitations as may be from time to time prescribed by the Club, and shall make a report of their proceedings at each annual meeting.

They shall appoint from their number a House Committee of three, who shall control the expenses and charges of the Club, regulate prices, receive and redress complaints, and have the immediate charge and superintendence of the Club and Club House, subject, however, at all times, to the direction of the Executive Committee.

The House Committee shall have power, subject always to the control of the Executive Committee, to engage and discharge the servants of the Club, and to make necessary purchases and sales.

The Executive Committee, of which five shall be a quorum, shall hold stated meetings during the first week of every month, — July, August, and September excepted, — for the transaction of business ; and special meetings may be called by the Secretary, on request of the President or any Vice-President, or of any two Directors, upon notice, printed or written, sent to each member at least twenty-four hours before the time appointed for such meeting.

The House Committee shall hold meetings on Monday evening of each week, at eight o'clock. The Chairman of the House Committee shall be exempt from payment of the annual assessment.

SECTION 6. After the first election of the Directors and Committee on Admissions, each annual election shall be for three Directors and three members of such committee, to hold office for three years, to supply the place of the class retiring that year, and for such additional number, if any, as may be necessary to fill vacancies, to hold office during the remainder of the terms of the members whose places they fill. At the first election, Directors shall be elected in three classes of three each, whose terms shall expire in one, two, and three years respectively.

SECTION 7. The Auditing Committee shall be elected annually, and shall consist of three persons, two of whom shall be a quorum. The duty of the Auditing Committee shall be to audit from time to time at its discretion the accounts of the Treasurer, and to present its report at each Annual Meeting.

SECTION 8. Any officer may be removed for cause, at a meeting of the Club, called for that purpose with two weeks' notice ; and a vacancy in any office, where not otherwise provided for, may be filled for the residue of the term by the Club at any meeting thereof. Neglect on the part of any member of a standing or special committee to attend three consecutive meetings of such committee shall be deemed a tender of his resignation of his office, which the committee may accept unless an explanation of such neglect, satisfactory to the committee, shall be given.

Standing Committees may fill vacancies in their membership.

No person shall serve on more than one of the standing committees, or hold more than one office in the Club, at the same time.

ARTICLE II.

MEMBERS.

SECTION 1. The Committee on Admissions shall consist of the Secretary and nine other members of the Club, five of whom shall constitute a quorum. Meetings of the committee shall be held on the first Tuesday after the first Saturday of every month, except July, August, and September.

The committee chosen in 1890 shall, at its first meeting, divide the elected members thereof, not including the Secretary, by lot or otherwise, into three classes of three each, the term of office of one class to expire at the annual meeting in 1891, of the second class at the same time in 1892, and of the third class at the same time in 1893. At each annual meeting after that of 1890 three new members of the committee shall be chosen for the term of three years, and the members whose term of office expires shall not be immediately eligible for reëlection.

Whenever any person shall be proposed for membership, written application must be made by a member of the Club to the Committee on Admissions, subscribed by him, setting forth the full name and occupation and place of residence of the person proposed, and the date of such proposal. If two thirds of the Committee after careful examination and consideration shall deem him a suitable person for membership, they shall cause his name to be placed on the notice board, as a candidate for admission, for the space of ten days.

All elections shall be by secret ballot: thirty votes shall be necessary to constitute a ballot on each nomination ; and one-fifth part of the votes cast, or more than twenty votes, being in the negative, shall constitute a rejection. The ballot-box shall be kept in the custody of the clerk at the office. Printed or written lists of the candidates to be balloted for shall be provided for the use of the members as ballots, which may be deposited in the box at any time after the nomination until the balloting shall be closed. Each member may write Yes or No against any names on his ballot ; and his vote shall not be counted for or against any candidate not thus marked. The balloting shall be closed at seven o'clock of the evening of the tenth day thereof, and the votes shall be counted by at least two members of the Executive Committee, who shall report to the Committee on Admissions the election or rejection of the candidate, and the Secretary shall enter the same on the records of the Club, and shall post on the notice-board a list of the candidates elected. No one but the committee who count the votes, the Secretary, and the clerk shall, on any account, see the list of members who have so voted, or be informed as to the proceedings of the committee, the votes cast, or the persons voting. No candidate who shall have been rejected shall be again proposed within six months.

Any person duly elected a member shall, upon signing the By-Laws, and paying an entrance-fee of twenty-five dollars and the annual assessment, or, if elected after the first day of October in any year, the entrance-fee and half of the annual assessment, become thenceforth entitled to all the rights and privileges of membership, provided such acts shall be performed within two months from the date of such election. Persons elected members of the Club during the month of March in any year shall not be required to pay any assessment for that financial year. The number of members at any one time shall not exceed four hundred.

Immediately after the election of a person to membership, the Secretary of the Club shall inform him of his election.

SECTION 2. If any person elected shall not,

within two months after notice of his election, left at or sent to his address, as specified by the member proposing him, signify his acceptance, and pay his admission fee and annual dues, he shall be deemed to have declined to become a member.

SECTION 3. All resignations shall be made, in writing, to the Executive Committee; but if made after the second Thursday of April, such resignations shall not discharge the member presenting it from his dues for the current year.

SECTION 4. If the conduct of a member shall appear to the Executive Committee to be disorderly, in violation of the rules, prejudicial to the interests or character of the Club, or contrary to its By-Laws, the committee shall inform him thereof in writing, and, if the nature of the offense in its opinion requires, request him to resign.

Such member shall have the right of appeal to the Club. The Club may expel such member by a vote, taken by ballot, of a majority of the members present at any business meeting.

SECTION 5. The fiscal year shall commence on the first day of April. The annual dues for members shall be thirty dollars, payable in advance on the first of April. If not paid within thirty days thereafter, it shall be the duty of the Treasurer to notify the delinquent member, and if such dues are not paid within twenty days after such notice, his name shall be posted by the Treasurer in a conspicuous place in the Club House ; and should he neglect payment, without good cause, until the first day of June, he shall thereupon cease to be a member.

All indebtedness of members to the Club, other than for assessments, shall be paid on or before the first day of every month. And if at the expiration of the fourteenth day of any month, any member shall not have paid his dues to the Club for the preceding month, he shall receive no further credit until such dues are paid. It shall be the duty of the clerk, upon the fifteenth day of each month, to post in some conspicuous place in the Club House the names of all members whose dues are then unpaid, together with the amount due from each member, there to remain until the same are paid. The Executive Committee may at any meeting declare forfeited the membership of any member whose name and the amount due from him having been posted as aforesaid shall have remained posted forty-five days, provided such amount or some part thereof shall remain unpaid at the time of such meeting.

SECTION 6. Any member who has paid an admission fee and the annual dues for one year, and who may be absent from the State for a continuous period of a year, shall be exempted from the payment of the annual dues for the period of his absence, provided he shall have given previous written notice to the Treasurer of his intention so to be absent.

SECTION 7. No dues or assessments other than those provided for in these By-Laws shall be levied, except by a two-thirds vote of members present at a regularly called meeting, the notice of which meeting shall state the subject to be considered.

SECTION 8. The Board of Directors first elected shall have the power to elect in such manner as they see fit not more than 287 members.

ARTICLE III.

STRANGERS.

SECTION 1. No person other than a member shall be admitted to the Club House, except by first entering his name, and that of the person introducing him, in a book kept for that purpose. Gentlemen residing within twenty miles of Cambridge may be introduced once in thirty days.

SECTION 2. Gentlemen residing out of the city of Cambridge, and having no usual place

of business or study within, shall be considered strangers, and any member of the Club may extend the privileges of the Club House, for not more than ten days, to any such stranger; but this privilege shall not be granted oftener than once in thirty days.

SECTION 3. The Executive Committee or the President may, at the request of any member, issue written invitations to strangers residing as aforesaid, for a period of thirty days, and may renew the same at discretion.

Any member who may avail himself of this privilege shall be held responsible for the payment of all debts or liabilities to the Club that may be incurred by any person introduced by him.

SECTION 4. Members may also invite gentlemen who are not members of the Club to private entertainments, in such rooms as may be designated for that purpose by the Executive Committee; and may introduce ladies to such rooms as may be appointed by the same committee.

Any member who may avail himself of these privileges shall be held responsible for the payment of all debts or liabilities to the Club that may be incurred by any person introduced by him.

ARTICLE IV.

NON-RESIDENT MEMBERS.

Persons having no customary place of abode, business, or study in Cambridge may be elected non-resident members as in the manner hereinbefore provided, and shall pay an admission fee of fifteen dollars and half the annual assessment. They shall not be entitled to vote or hold office, nor shall they have any interest in the property of the Club.

ARTICLE V.

SEAL OF THE CLUB.

The Seal of the Club shall bear the inscription "THE COLONIAL CLUB, CAMBRIDGE, MASS., INCORPORATED 1890."

ARTICLE VI.

OF MEETINGS.

SECTION 1. The Annual Meeting of the Club after 1890 shall be held at eight o'clock P. M., on the first Monday of April, for the election of officers and the transaction of such other business as may come before it. The

Annual Meeting of 1890 shall take place on the first Monday of June.

At the monthly meeting of the Executive Committee in March of each year, a committee of seven shall be appointed by it from members of the Club not members of the Executive Committee or of the Committee on Admissions, who shall select, notify the Secretary of the Club, and post in a conspicuous place in the Club House, at least ten days before the Annual Meeting, the name of a candidate for each office to be filled at the ensuing annual election. It shall be the duty of the Secretary to have printed ballots prepared for the Annual Meeting.

SECTION 2. A quorum of one tenth of the whole number of members of the Club shall be requisite for the transaction of business at any meeting of the Club.

SECTION 3. Special meetings of the Club may be called at any time by order of the President, with the approval of three members of the Executive Committee, and shall be called by the Secretary whenever the President or any Vice-President shall be thereunto requested in writing by twenty-five members, setting forth the purpose of such meeting. At any such special meeting, no business, other than that specified in the call, shall be considered.

SECTION 4. At the meetings of the Club, the order of business, so far as the character and nature of the meeting may admit, shall be as follows : —

1. Reading the minutes of the last meeting.
2. Report of Executive Committee.
3. Reports of Standing Committees.
4. Reports of Special Committees.
5. Report of the Treasurer.
6. Report of the Secretary.
7. Election of Officers.
8. General business.

But this order of business may be changed by a majority of the meeting.

SECTION 5. Any motion or resolution offered for the consideration of the Club shall, at the request of any member, be reduced to writing before it is acted upon.

All special committees for any purpose shall be appointed by the presiding officer, unless otherwise ordered, and a majority thereof shall not be members of the Executive Committee.

SECTION 6. No person not a member of the Club shall be present at any business meeting thereof unless specially invited by the Executive Committee.

ARTICLE VII.

HOUSE RULES.

The House Committee shall enforce the following House Rules, and also make and enforce such other House Rules as they may from time to time find necessary for the welfare of the Club : —

I. No person shall take from the Club House a newspaper, pamphlet, book, or other article the property of the club, nor mutilate, deface, or destroy the same.

II. Books, pamphlets, and newspapers shall not be removed from the reading and drawing rooms.

III. No member shall give any money or gratuity to a servant of the club.

IV. No rooms in the house shall be let, nor shall any room be closed to any member, except by the order of the House Committee.

V. The Club House shall be closed for the admission of members as early as one o'clock A. M. on each day.

VI. No gambling shall be allowed in the club.

VII. No dogs shall be allowed in the Club House.

VIII. A reasonable charge shall be made for the use of card and billiard tables.

IX.   No games shall be allowed in the Club House from twelve o'clock on Saturday evening until its opening on Monday morning, or while any meeting of the club is in session.

X.   During a business meeting of the Club no smoking shall be allowed in the room where the meeting is held.

XI.   Smoking will not be permitted in the Library at any time, or in the Dining Room until after nine o'clock P. M.

XII.   Private Dining Rooms cannot be assigned to parties numbering less than four persons.

ARTICLE VIII.

AMENDMENT OF BY-LAWS.

Any By-Law of the Club may be amended, or a new By-Law made, at any regular meeting of the Club, the proposer having posted upon the notice-board notice of the proposed alteration or addition, for at least thirty days immediately preceding said meeting, and the Secretary having sent notice by mail to each member at least ten days before said meeting, when, if two thirds of those present and voting shall vote in favor of the proposed alteration or amendment, the same shall be adopted.

OFFICERS

1890.

President.
THOMAS WENTWORTH HIGGINSON.

Vice-Presidents.
CHARLES W. ELIOT.   E D. LEAVITT.
CHESTER W. KINGSLEY.   EDMUND REARDON.

Secretary.
GEO. HOWLAND COX.

Treasurer.
EDMUND A. WHITMAN.

Board of Directors.
HENRY P. WALCOTT.   GARDINER M. LANE.
CHESTER F SANGER.   JAMES J. MYERS.
CHARLES J. McINTIRE.   FRANCIS V. B. KERN.
EDGAR R. CHAMPLIN.   CHARLES C. FOSTER.
HENRY E. WARNER.

OFFICERS

1891.

President.

THOMAS WENTWORTH HIGGINSON.

Vice-Presidents.

CHARLES W. ELIOT.	CHESTER W. KINGSLEY.
HENRY P. WALCOTT.	E. D. LEAVITT.

Secretary.

GEO. HOWLAND COX.

Treasurer.

EDMUND A. WHITMAN.

Board of Directors.

ALBERT F. HARLOW.	H. O. HOUGHTON, JR.
CHARLES L. FULLER.	BANCROFT G. DAVIS.
GARDINER M. LANE.	CHESTER F. SANGER.
JAMES J. MYERS.	CHARLES J. McINTIRE.

FRANCIS V. B. KERN.

OFFICERS

1892.

President.

THOMAS WENTWORTH HIGGINSON.

Vice-Presidents.

CHARLES W. ELIOT.   E. D. LEAVITT.

CHESTER W. KINGSLEY.   HENRY P. WALCOTT.

Secretary.

GEO. HOWLAND COX.

Treasurer.

EDMUND A. WHITMAN.

Board of Directors.

JAMES J. MYERS.   BANCROFT G. DAVIS.

ALVIN F. SORTWELL.   GARDINER M. LANE.

CHARLES R. SHAW.   ALBERT F. HARLOW.

H. O. HOUGHTON, JR.   CHARLES L. FULLER.

OFFICERS

1893.

President.

CHARLES W. ELIOT.

Vice-Presidents.

RICHARD H. DANA.   ARTHUR E. DENISON.
JOHN W. HAMMOND.   CHARLES J. McINTIRE.

Secretary.

GEO. HOWLAND COX.

Treasurer.

EDMUND A. WHITMAN.

Board of Directors.

GEORGE A. BARTLETT.   ALVIN F. SORTWELL.
HERBERT A. CHASE.   CHARLES R. SHAW.
EDWIN B. HALE.   H. O. HOUGHTON, Jr.
JAMES J. MYERS.   ALBERT F. HARLOW.
CHARLES L. FULLER.

OFFICERS

1894.

President.

CHARLES W. ELIOT.

Vice-Presidents.

RICHARD H. DANA.   ARTHUR E. DENISON.
JOHN W. HAMMOND.   CHARLES J. McINTIRE.

Secretary.

GEO. HOWLAND COX.

Treasurer.

EDMUND A. WHITMAN.

Directors.

To serve till April, 1895.

JAMES J. MYERS.   CHARLES R. SHAW.
ALVIN F. SORTWELL.

To serve till April, 1896.

GEORGE A. BARTLETT.   EDWIN B. HALE.
HERBERT A. CHASE.

To serve till April, 1897.

PHILIP S. ABBOTT   ASA M. MATTICE.
GEORGE P. JOHNSON.

Committee on Admissions.

To serve till April, 1895,

WM. M. RICHARDSON.   RUSSELL BRADFORD.
HENRY B. DAVIS.

To serve till April, 1896.

J. BERTRAM WILLIAMS.   FRANCIS E. SEAVER.
EDWIN P. BOGGS.

To serve till April, 1897.

WATSON G. CUTTER. HERBERT PUTNAM.
BANCROFT G. DAVIS.

Auditing Committee.

WM. T. PIPER. GEORGE A. ALLISON.
JOHN C. BULLARD.

House Committee.

ALVIN F. SORTWELL, Chairman.
GEORGE A. BARTLETT. ASA M. MATTICE.

Committee on Library and Publications.

T. W. HIGGINSON, Chairman.
HENRY O. HOUGHTON, Jr. CHARLES J. PETERS.

Committee on Entertainment.

ANDREW McFARLAND DAVIS, Chairman.
JUSTIN WINSOR. ALBERT F. HARLOW.

LIST OF MEMBERS

Complete to Oct. 1, 1894. Members will please send corrections to the Secretary.

A

EDWIN H. ABBOT
PHILIP STANLEY ABBOT
FREDERICK D. ALLEN
W. FRANK ALLEY
GEORGE A. ALLISON
ALBERT F. AMEE
JOHN AMEE
JAMES BARR AMES
ROBERT R. ANDREWS
JOHN H. APPLETON

B

ARVID BAALACK
FRANCIS W. BACON
M. CLINTON BACON
HOLLIS R. BAILEY
WILDER D. BANCROFT
WALWORTH O. BARBOUR
FRANCIS J. BARNES
GEORGE A. BARTLETT
EDWARD L. BEARD
JOSIAH Q. BENNETT
E. SIDNEY BERRY
ALEX. H. BILL
CLARENCE H. BILLINGS
CHARLES C. BLANEY
STEPHEN H. BLODGETT

WARREN K. BLODGETT, JR.
EDWIN P. BOGGS
AUSTIN D. BOSS
WILLIAM F. BRADBURY
RUSSELL BRADFORD
GEORGE E. BRIGHAM
ELMER H. BRIGHT
JOHN BROOKS
JOHN GRAHAM BROOKS
J. MASON BROOKS
SUMNER A. BROOKS
LEROY S. BROWN
OTIS S. BROWN
SILAS E. BUCK
JOHN C. BULLARD
H. PRESCOTT BURLEIGH

C

LUCIEN CARR
CHARLES T. CARRUTH
MONTAGUE CHAMBERLAIN
EDGAR R. CHAMPLIN
GILBERT E. CHANDLER
GEORGE S. CHASE
HERBERT A. CHASE
LOUIS S. CHASE
EDWARD R. COGSWELL
GEORGE H. CONVERSE
FRANK GAYLORD COOK
ARCHIBALD C. COOLIDGE
JOHN H. CORCORAN
WILLIAM F. CORNE
SAMUEL F. COUES
ROBERT COWEN
GEO. HOWLAND COX
MATT. H. CRAWFORD
JOHN M. CROCKER
SIMON G. CROSWELL

FRED L. CUNNINGHAM
JOHN L. CURRIE
CHARLES F. CUSHMAN
GEORGE W. CUSHMAN
RUFUS C. CUSHMAN
FRANK B. CUTTER
HENRY O. CUTTER
WATSON G. CUTTER

D

RICHARD H. DANA
E. A. DAVENPORT
ANDREW McF. DAVIS
BANCROFT G. DAVIS
HENRY B. DAVIS
JAMES HENRY DAVIS
ARTHUR E. DENISON
JOHN O. DE WOLF
DAVID T. DICKINSON
CHARLES W. DIMICK
EDWARD S. DODGE
WILLIAM W. DODGE
GEORGE B. DORR
JOHN C. DOW
EDWIN DRESSER
WILLIAM B. DURANT
OLIVER H. DURRELL

E

WALTER F. EARLE
RICHARD ELA
WALTER ELA
CHARLES W. ELIOT
EMMONS R. ELLIS
HARRY ELLIS
STEARNS R. ELLIS
WILLIAM R. ELLIS
HENRY ENDICOTT

CHARLES J. ENEBUSKE
ALBERT S. EUSTIS
CHARLES C. EVERETT
EDWARD F. EVERETT

F

WILLIAM G. FARLOW
CHARLES R. FARRINGTON
WELLINGTON FILLMORE
FREDERICK P. FISH
GEORGE W. FITZ.
CHARLES C. FOSTER
FRANCIS C. FOSTER
JABEZ FOX
DANIEL E. FRAZIER
CHARLES L. FULLER

G

GEORGE W. GALE
THOMAS B. GANNETT
JOHN L. GARDNER, 2D
LEWIS EDWARD GATES
ARTHUR GILMAN
GEORGE M. GLAZIER
GUSTAVUS GOEPPER
WILLIAM GOEPPER
GEORGE L. GOODALE
FREEMAN C. GOODNOW
ARTHUR GORDON GOODRICH
CHARLES H. GRANDGENT
LEVI R. GREENE
JAMES B. GREENOUGH
WILLIAM M. GRISWOLD
WALTER C. GROVER

H

EDWIN B. HALE
CHARLES G. HALEY

WILLIAM C. HALL
JOHN W. HAMMOND
LEANDER M. HANNUM
PAUL H. HANUS
ALBERT F. HARLOW
CHARLES HARRIS
FRANK W. HASTINGS
LEWIS M. HASTINGS
SOLON S. HASTINGS
ARTHUR GILLESPIE HATCH
JAMES W. HAYWOOD
JAMES W. HAZEN
JOHN J. HENDERSON
JOHN O. HENSHAW
THOMAS WENTWORTH HIGGINSON
JOHN L. HILDRETH
STANLEY B. HILDRETH
ADAMS S. HILL
FRANK A. HILL
F. STANHOPE HILL
HENRY B. HILL
WILLIAM H. HILL
WILLIAM B. HILLS
JAMES HENRY HILTON
IRA N. HOLLIS
EDWARD W. HOOPER
JOHN HOPEWELL, JR.
FRED. W. HOPKINS
EDWARD R. HOUGHTON
HENRY O. HOUGHTON
HENRY O. HOUGHTON, JR.
ARTHUR L. HOWARD
ARCHIBALD M. HOWE
FRED C. HOWE
GEORGE E. HOWE
BENJAMIN L. HOWES
EUGENE L. HOWLETT
RAY GREENE HULING

FREEMAN HUNT
THOMAS HUNT
OLIVER HUNTINGTON
BYRON S. HURLBURT
DANA W. HYDE
WM. A. HUNNEWELL

J

CHARLES L. JACKSON
ROBERT TREAT JACKSON
WILLIAM JAMES
GEORGE P. JOHNSON
HENRY WALTER JONES

K

STILLMAN F. KELLEY
FREDERICK KENDALL :
OLINDUS F. KENDALL
FRANK A. KENNEDY
FRANCIS V. B. KERN
CHESTER W. KINGSLEY
GEORGE LYMAN KITTRIDGE

L

ROLAND O. LAMB
WILLIAM B. LAMBERT
GEORGE H. LAWRENCE
WILLIAM LAWRENCE
E. D. LEAVITT
GRANVILLE B. LENFEST
GEORGE V. LEVERETT
JOSEPH P. LIVERMORE
HENRY A. LOCKE
EUGENE R. LUKE
WALTER J. LUKE

M

RUFUS H. MANSON
PHILIPPE B. MARCOU
ALFRED R. MARSH
M. SYLVESTER MARSHALL
ASA M. MATTICE
CHARLES J. McINTIRE
HERBERT B. McINTIRE
ALEXANDER McKENZIE
JAMES MELLEN
ALLYNE L. MERRILL
GEORGE S. MERRILL
STUART C. MILLER
CHARLES H. MONTAGUE
GEORGE A. MOORE
F. MORELAND
EDWIN V. MORGAN
GEORGE F. MORGAN
MORRIS H. MORGAN
CHARLES H. MORSE
CHARLES W. MUNROE
WILLIAM A. MUNROE
HUGO MÜNSTERBERG
JAMES J. MYERS

N

BENNETT H. NASH
GEORGE A. NASH
WILLIAM H. NEAL
WILLIAM W. NEWELL
ALFRED B. NICHOLS
EDGAR H. NICHOLS
JOHN T. G. NICHOLS
JAMES ATKINS NOYES

O

JOHN L. ODIORNE
WILLIAM D. ORCUTT

P

ALFRED P. PAGE
JAMES L. PAINE
JOHN K. PAINE
HENRY A. PARKER
FRANCIS G. PEABODY
JAMES MILLS PEIRCE
ASA E. PERVERE
CHARLES J. PETERS
G. A. A. PEVEY
E. BURT PHILLIPS
CHARLES E. PIERCE
WILLIAM TAGGARD PIPER
EUGENE A. POPE
ALFRED C. POTTER
WALLACE PREBLE
DAVID PROUDFOOT
FREDERICK W. PUTNAM
HERBERT PUTNAM

R

ALBERT H. RANLET
EDMUND REARDON
JAMES F. RHODES
JAMES B. RICE, JR.
REUBEN FRANCIS RICHARDS
THEODORE WM. RICHARDS
WILLIAM M. RICHARDSON
DAVID A. RITCHIE
WILL F. ROAF
BENJ. R. ROBINSON
EDWARD C. ROBINSON
CHARLES J. ROLFE

DENMAN W. ROSS
WILLIAM J. ROUNDS
JOSIAH ROYCE
CHARLES THEO. RUSSELL, JR.
J. HENRY RUSSELL
GEORGE H. RYTHER

S

GEORGE SANTAYANA
DUDLEY A. SARGENT
WILLIAM B. SAUL
GEORGE E. SAUNDERS
ENOS D. SAWYER
GEORGE A. SAWYER
JOHN S. SAWYER
SAMUEL H. SCUDDER
WINTHROP SALTONSTALL SCUDDER
FRANCIS E. SEAVER
NATHANIEL S. SHALER
ADNA B. SHAW
CHARLES R. SHAW
WILLIAM L. SHEARER
EDWARD C. SHERBURNE
SAMUEL S. SIAS
JOHN SIMPKINS
SOLOMON S. SLEEPER
CHAUNCEY SMITH
CHAUNCEY SMITH, JR.
CLEMENT L. SMITH
FREDERICK M. SMITH
JEREMIAH SMITH
ALVIN F. SORTWELL
WILLIAM P. SOULE
HERBERT F. SPARROW
CHARLES H. STEVENS
EDMUND H. STEVENS
HAROLD W. STEVENS
JOHN LYMAN STONE

WILLIAM E. STONE
FLAVEL C. STRATTON
FREDERICK C. DE SUMICHRAST
RANDOLPH C. SURBRIDGE
WILLIAM D. SWAN

T

FREDERICK W. TAYLOR
JOHN LEWIS TAYLOR
FRANK H. TEELE
WM. R. THAYER
JOSEPH G. THORP
JOSEPH G. THORP, JR.
THOMAS B. TICKNOR
HENRY N. TILTON
JOSEPH TORREY, JR.
CRAWFORD H. TOY
ALFRED T. TURNER, JR.
DANIEL LAWRENCE TURNER

U

SAMUEL USHER

V

A. ABBOTT VAUGHAN
BENJAMIN VAUGHAN
CHARLES E. VAUGHAN
FRANCIS W. VAUGHAN

W

ENOCH H. WAKEFIELD, JR.
HENRY P. WALCOTT
ROBERT DeCOURCY WARD
EDWARD J. WARDWELL
FRANK W. WARDWELL
CHARLES F. WARNER
JOSEPH B. WARNER
HENRY C. WARREN

H. LANGFORD WARREN
ALFRED FOSTER WASHBURN
ASHLEY WATSON
JOHN C. WATSON
JAMES A. WELLS
BARRETT WENDELL
WALTER WESSELHOEFT
EDWARD C. WHEELER
HENRY N. WHEELER
CHARLES J. WHITE
HENRY WHITE
HERBERT H. WHITE
JOHN WILLIAMS WHITE
MOSES P. WHITE
STEPHEN B. WHITING
EDMUND A. WHITMAN
WILLIAM H. WHITNEY
CHARLES A. WHITTEMORE
FRED W. WHITTEMORE
RAYMOND S. WILDER
J. BERTRAM WILLIAMS
ROBERT W. WILLSON
C. F. WILSON
JUSTIN WINSOR
WILLIAM H. WOOD
HARRY J. WOOD
CHARLES R. WOODS
JAMES A. WOOLSON
GEORGE G. WRIGHT
MORRILL WYMAN, JR.

Y

HENRY D. YERXA

Z

FRANK ZINKEISEN

NON-RESIDENTS

ISAAC ADAMS...................Annisquam
SMITH BAKER...................
JONATHAN BIGELOW...........
CLARENCE JOHN BLAKE......Boston
CHARLES S. CLARK.............Boston
ADOLPHE COHN................New York
EDWARD COWLES..............Somerville
ALLEN DANFORTH.............Boston
FREDERIC DODGE.............Belmont
WALLACE S. DRAPER..........Boston
FRANKLIN G. FESSENDEN.....Greenfield
J. B. FLETCHER.................
WYMAN K. FLINT..............Milwaukee
BENJ. IVES GILMAN............Boston
WM. B. HAND...................Nyack, N. Y.
CHARLES H. HAPGOOD........Chicago, Ill.
THEODORE P. HARDING......Boston
EDWARD D. HOOKER..........Arlington
RICHARD HITTINGER.........Belmont
GEORGE G. KENNEDY.........Roxbury
WALDO LINCOLN...............Worcester
CHARLES A. LOCKE...........Chestnut Hill
WM. L. MERCER................Somerville
GORDON McKAY................Newport, R. I.
GEORGE O. MORGAN...........Pittsburgh, Penn.
PALMER ELLIS PRESBREY....Brookline
GEORGE PUTNAM..............Boston
GEORGE M. RICHARDSON......Berkeley, Cal.
EDWIN P. SEAVER.............Newton
PARKER F. SOULE.............Boston
FREDERICK H. VIAUX.........Boston
F. C. WOODMAN................New York

In Memoriam

CHESTER F. SANGER...Died November,   1891
HENRY H. GILMORE.... " December 24, "
MAX RADER............ " April   1, 1892
DR. WM. B. FISKE ...... " May   8, "
REUBEN AREY......... " July   7, "
ALBERT A. REDWAY... " July   24, "
SAMUEL LONGFELLOW. " October   3, "
EBEN N. HORSFORD.... " January   1, 1893
SUMNER ALBEE......... " January 12, "
HENRY R. GLOVER...... " May   28, "
WILLIAM R. HOWLAND. " April   25, "
GEN. E. W. HINCKS...... " February 14, 1894
DR. FREEMAN SNOW.... " September 11, "
JOSIAH PARSONS COOKE " September 3, "